D1736185

How a Goat Became Mayor and the Political Spring That Followed

Authored by: Ricco Garcia & Samuel Garcia

Contributor: Carlos Pena

Foreword by Nino Monea

Edited by James Willard & Wendy Chu

Research assisted by James Willard

Cover Photo by Giorgia Basso

Special Thanks

We would like to thank everybody who helped out by either editing, helping us brainstorm, or by giving us their honest opinions on topics we were writing about. We would also like to thank our incredible family for helping so much along the way. We seriously could not have done this without all of your help.

We would like to dedicate this book to our late father. We know you're looking down on us from Heaven. We think about you every day. Love you big guy.

"For the commandment *is* a lamp; and the law *is* light; and reproofs of instruction *are* the way of life."

Proverbs 6:23

Foreword

In one sense, I came to know Sam Garcia before I ever met him. In February of 2015, I was at a conference at the University of Texas – Austin. As is my habit at every college I visit, I picked up the school newspaper to browse through. On the front page, I saw a bizarre pair of men. One of them had his shirt almost entirely unbuttoned, and the other one had a look of utter bewilderment on his face. Turns out the duo—Xavier Rotnofsky and Rohit Mandalapu—had just been elected student body president and vice president of UT. Their campaign was viewed as a joke at the beginning, but they went on to address real issues on campus. Little did I know that Sam played a pivotal role in the election: he hosted an event (featuring goats, of course) that was a breakout moment for the unlikely campaign. Were it not for the event, I may have read a very different article on that February morning.

Fast forward a couple of years, and I had the chance to meet Sam face-to-face. He started as a first-year student at Harvard Law School, where I serve as Student Body President and Editor-in-Chief of the Harvard Journal on Legislation. While most first year law students are barely able to stay on top of their readings for class (myself included), Sam was more ambitious. He came to me seeking help in starting a new law journal, one that would focus on the law of addiction—the first of its kind in the nation. Needless to say, I was impressed.

Sam and his brother Ricco continue to impress with this book. Its timing could not be more opportune. The election of Donald Trump has left half the country desperately searching for an explanation for his victory. How could all of the polls, and all of the experts, been so wrong? This book provides a clear framework for understanding upset elections, from the White House to city hall. Although many of the reproachable actions Donald Trump took in the course of his campaign and administration have no precedent, his election was not the first time that the experts have gotten it completely wrong.

In 1948, for example, President Harry Truman launched what most considered a doomed reelection campaign. Pollsters declared his opponent Thomas Dewey "unbeatable" and stopped conducting surveys because the results appeared so obvious. The press corps was nearly unanimous in their pessimism. Professional gambling odds were 15 or 30-to-1 against the president. Three weeks before the election, Newsweek conducted a survey of 50 highly regarded political experts, and every single one predicted a Truman defeat.

But "Give 'em Hell Harry" was a fighter. He took to the campaign trail like no president before or since. He traveled tens of thousands of miles by train at a breakneck speed of 80 mph and saw millions. In contrast, his opponent's campaign offered "no surprises, and took no risks" in the words of historian David McCullough. In the end, Truman won a resounding victory. He captured 303 electoral votes, and won the popular vote by over two million.

Dewey's decision to "take no risks" ultimately backfired. And throughout history, presidents have found great success by leveraging the newest technology of the day. FDR used radio to speak intimately with millions of Americans. JFK recognized the importance of presenting a crisp image for the dynamic new medium of television. LBJ pioneered the use of helicopter campaigning to reach voters in rural Texas. The rapid pace of technological evolution today gives upstart candidates a real chance to take on the establishment.

Americans have a greater need to innovate than most. It's in our DNA. Our Constitution redefined idea of self-government and our nation's founding was an innovation on a historic scale. An ill-funded, ill-trained, and ill-equipped rebel army managed to overcome the most powerful empire in the world. It wasn't brute strength that carried the day, but tactical brilliance. From Henry Knox's audacious plan to transport a convoy of cannons in the dead of winter to George Washington's daring midnight assault at Battle of Trenton, innovation is as essential to a military campaign as to a political one.

I myself am no stranger to these lessons. Over the years, I have worked or volunteered on state, local, and national campaigns all around the country. Some of them have been successful, some of them have not. Throughout it all, I have seen that it is not enough to have money or institutional support. If candidates don't understand their voters, find good data, or innovate in the face of change, their campaign is nothing more than an intro to their own concession speech. Because in politics, the decision to "take no risks" can end up being the riskiest decision of all.

-Nino Monea
Student Body President
Harvard Law School

About The Authors and Contributors

Ricco Garcia

Hey I'm Ricco Garcia, some people may know me as "The only Detroit Lions fan in Texas", well at least until my little brother gets back home, but I usually go by Ricco. I'm currently an attorney out of Austin, Tx, but was born and raised in South Texas in a city named Mission. I went to undergrad at the University of Texas at Austin where I received a degree in Government, then went to law school at the University of Houston Law Center, finishing my final semester at Georgetown Law Center in D.C. I'm incredibly passionate about campaigns and policy (but in this book we'll stick strictly to campaigns, no soapboxes here), in fact if I'm known for anything else other than being an out of place Lions fan, it's my passion for the political process in general. My friends from back in the Rio Grande Valley can attest to this, in high school I went around registering every senior to vote in the '08 presidential election, prompting the local newspaper to write a story about me titled, "Citizen Garcia." I have worked two full legislative sessions at the Texas Capitol (in Texas "session" is a badge of honor) and am currently working in my third session as a Legislative Director/General Counsel. On top of my Texas experience I have had two stints working at the

United States Capitol in Washington D.C., most recently working with Congressman Joaquin Castro. The most relevant work experience, particularly to this book, is my campaign experience—much of which I would consider informal. I have worked campaigns across South Texas to Houston, and loved them all. This campaign experience has not been shouldered alone, most campaign work was shared with my little brother. When we were kids our Mom was a campaign manager for local elections as well as a Councilwoman herself, so Sam and I learned early on what block-walking was. The opportunity to write a book on a topic I am so deeply passionate about is incredible, but the chance to do so alongside my brother is a blessing.

Samuel Garcia

Hi! I'm Samuel Garcia, known to some as Ricco's little brother and to others as "that one dude who really likes goats or something", but I prefer to go by Sam! I am currently a student at Harvard Law School and before I came to law school I received my undergraduate degree from the Business Honors Program at the University of Texas at Austin. I grew up in South Texas (in particular Mission, Tx) and as a kid I was an actual goat herder for 6 years (forcing Ricco to do it with me at times). I finally put my goat knowledge to use during my time at UT Austin when

I wrote *How Goats Can Fight Poverty*, which went onto become an overnight bestseller! I went onto give a TEDx talk that conveniently has the same name as the book. During my senior year of college I began to work as the Chief Content Officer for a startup called HeartWater. My whole responsibility at this job was to write the daily stories and plot the general direction of the content. After a few months, and hundreds of stories, I decided to write a book called *Launching Point* with a number of my favorite stories, and a few personal ones. This book also became an overnight bestseller and now I am really excited to finally write my first book with my brother about a topic that we are both very passionate about!

Contributor- Carlos Pena

Hi there! My name is Carlos Pena. I was raised between Reynosa, Mexico and Mission, Texas. Throughout my life I've worked in many campaigns on both sides of the border. Growing up, I was always intrigued by the political environment that surrounded the US-Mexico border. At 18, I was fortunate enough to obtain a golf scholarship to attend George Washington University, where I graduated from the Honors Program and double majored in Political Science and International Affairs/Conflict Resolution. During my four awesome years at GW, I was able to intern in both the U.S. and Mexican Congresses, participating in the health, energy, and security committees. While in D.C. I volunteered at the DC Employment Justice Center, where I worked as a legal translator for Latin-American day laborers. In Mexico, I have done social work in the highlands of Chiapas and Oaxaca, organizing medical brigades in the most impoverished communities in Mexico. Nowadays, I serve as the President of the Desarrollo Integral de la Familia (DIF) (Family Development Department) of Reynosa, Mexico, where I supervise and develop different programs in order to help Reynosa citizens fully develop themselves and their families. The services my agency provides include 45 social programs, academic scholarships, health services, legal services, nutrition advising, education seminars, women empowerment classes, business seminars, student seminars, **senior benefits, disability benefits, low income benefits**, transportation for the disabled, physical and psychological therapy to thousands of citizens in our rehab center, meals to more than 11,000 kids every week, transportation for burn victims to Shriners hospital in Houston, housing for unaccompanied and undocumented minors after their detention and before their deportation, and the city orphanage. All of these programs fall under the DIF's responsibility and jurisdiction.

Translator- Diana Marin-Melo

My name is Diana Marin-Melo and I'm a junior at Georgetown University majoring in Government and Latin American History and pursuing a Certificate in Latin American Studies. I'm currently the Vice-President of the Georgetown Mexican Student Association and a fellow at Georgetown's Latin American Initiative, where I research illicit markets in Latin America like petroleum theft in Mexico. I've lived both in Mexico and the United States, and my engagement with DC includes employment with the Georgetown Center for Social Justice and volunteer positions at the DC Employment Justice Center, where I work as a legal translator for Latin-American day laborers.

Preface

At 11 pm on Election Night, my little brother (and co-author) called me. I hesitated to pick up the phone because I knew what the call was about. When I answered he described the scene at his law school following Hillary Clinton's probable loss as one of total despair. Every pollster said this could not happen, but here we were – watching Donald Trump successfully pull off one of the biggest political upsets of all time.

The next day reality sank in, and my brother and I were on the phone once again, but this time the conversation was different. We were discussing just how this happened, and researching whether there were examples in history that could explain this phenomenon. What we found is that results like the 2016 presidential election had happened before and at all levels of government from mayoral races to races for the White House.

In our research and analysis we found there are many ways a politician can be upset by their opponent, such as not understanding their electorate properly, lack of data, or being outmaneuvered technology wise (failing to innovate). Ultimately, we discovered that there is no set way to win an election, *but by not changing from past styles incumbents and new candidates alike guarantee an eventual loss.* To demonstrate this point, we will walk through goat mayor Clay Henry's election, Jesse Ventura's rise to governorship, Barack Obama's election, Donald Trump's campaign points, an exclusive look into how the PAN took the Mexican state of Tamaulipas from the PRI written by the President of DIF Reynosa, and many other upset elections.

Clay Henry: The G.O.A.T. Politician

As the sun rises in West Texas, the morning dew begins to dry off the grave of former Lajitas mayor, Clay Henry. Clay Henry became a legend by setting out to run a campaign that was inherently different from his competition. After Clay Henry's victory, a political dynasty was started as the position of mayor of Lajitas was passed on from father to son. However, there were people who opposed the Clay Henry Dynasty. A local man named Jim Bob Hargrove grew jealous of Clay Henry III and one day viciously attacked and castrated Clay Henry III. He was caught soon after and brought up on charges. Unfortunately, Clay Henry Sr.'s life was cut short after a fight with his son, Clay Henry Jr., ended up taking his life. I wouldn't be too sad for Clay Henry Sr. since this is a decently natural way for him to pass away.

This is because Clay Henry Sr. is a goat.

Lajitas, TX- nestled in the southern region of Brewster County, this tiny community was set to have a small vote with huge implications. During one of the first elections for mayor, a Houstonian named Tommy Steele ran and won.[1] The election of a

---

[1]https://www.nationalparkreservations.com/article/lajitas-mayor-clay-henry/

Houstonian to mayor in a community roughly 667 miles away from Houston upset a local named Bill Ivey. Ivey went on to say if someone from Houston could be mayor, then his goat could be mayor. So Bill Ivey put up Clay Henry to run against Tommy Steele in the next election under the slogan "You just have to give a darn." Tommy Steele ran under the promise of getting Lajitas a snow plow, which would be virtually useless considering the town averages .1 inches of snowfall a year.

The change in campaigning Clay Henry brought proved to be too much for the Houstonian, and in a decisive victory Clay Henry took his rightful throne as the mayor of Lajitas, Texas. If you are from Texas, you may have heard that Clay Henry had something going for him outside of a dashing goatee and an impressive set of horns. Clay Henry could, not kidding, drink between 35-40 beers a day, and was widely known as the beer drinking goat.[2]

It may be almost too easy to pass this election off as a joke or an anomaly, because why would anyone ever truly want a goat as mayor? However, this is not the first time that this has happened. In the sleepy California town of Anza, an election was held for mayor and a goat named Opie was elected.[3] There

[2] http://www.roadsideamerica.com/story/2227
[3] http://articles.latimes.com/2005/nov/30/local/me-

is no record that Opie's party skills were as developed as Lajitas mayor, Clay Henry, but the goat did have an avid following. In fact, when there was an attempt to take Opie out of office, the citizens of Anza fought back and argued to keep Opie in office. You might be thinking to yourself: "Why why why?"

There was something that drew voters to elect goats over actual human beings. If you skipped the "About the Authors", no judging, you may have missed that my brother and I have experience with goats. Sam was a goat herder for 6 years and even went onto write a bestselling book called *How Goats Can Fight Poverty*, but even we will admit, that the smartest goat is less qualified to lead than any normal person (shocking, we know). However, this does not mean that electing a person will technically deliver results more in line with what a particular voter wants. In the two cases outlined in this chapter, many of the people in those towns believed that a goat would best deliver what they wanted over an actual person. Despite the strangeness of their choice, we believe that the people who elected Clay Henry and Opie were acting reasonably.

opie30

Every Voter is Reasonable

There are a number of ways that academia has tried to rationalize human behavior, but what if we are actually all reasonable in our own way?

The study of economics suggests that there is an objectively reasonable way for humans to act. By economic standards, someone is acting reasonably, if they calculate all options when making a decision and pick the one with the highest payback or the lowest cost. However, you can just imagine the incalculable number of options available to a person when they are making any given decision.

In law school, every student is introduced to the "reasonable man". The "reasonable man" is an objective standard used by courts to determine whether someone was acting reasonably when performing a certain action. Courts will use this standard when deciding issues like whether a person could have reasonably foreseen that something would occur. For example, could a reasonable person have foreseen that if they didn't salt their icy patio, then a person could slip on the icy tile? The "reasonable man" is often criticized by law students, lawyers, and people in general for being largely unrealistic. This is because the view on how the "reasonable man" should act is often tainted with a large amount of hindsight. We would imagine that the law school version of the reasonable man is someone who drives 5 mph under the speed limit at all times, eats the same thing for every meal, is in bed by 7 every night, and is not exactly the life of every party.

If you used either of these two standards to measure whether a person is reasonable, you would think that people as a whole are the most irrational species on the planet. However, we believe that every voter is in their own way reasonable since they have reasoning that is valid to them, even if their logic makes no sense to us. In fact, we believe that looking at people in this way is the only way to break down barriers and truly understand each other.

In the Lajitas election for mayor, there were a number of people who actually went out of their way to vote in a goat as mayor, and a number that voted for the other candidate. We believe that both sides were acting reasonably since they had valid intentions behind their votes. At the time of the mayoral election, Lajitas was close to becoming a ghost town. Anyone going out of their way to vote for mayor wanted their vote to say and do certain things. The people who voted for the person in the election were hoping that maybe something would turn around while riding the status quo. The people who voted for the goat, Clay Henry, had something very different in mind. Those voters wanted to voice their apathy about the condition of the community with a joke protest vote, and their voices were heard loud and clear.[4]

In the minds of the people who voted for Clay Henry, a vote for a person was useless. A vote for Clay Henry, was worth more to them since it told the local government that they were so sick of the status quo, and that they would rather nothing be done at all than stick with it.

Perhaps an even better example of voters reacting to the status quo can be found thousands of miles away from Lajitas, in the small community of Anza, California. In Anza, the race for mayor is a charity competition, so instead of the candidate with the most votes winning it is actually the candidate who raises the most money. The mayoral race in Anza featured four different candidates, one of whom was the incumbent mayor, Carl Long, and a new challenger, Opie the Goat. Considering that there was actually an incumbent running, one can imagine that this race would be no walk in the pasture for Opie. Opie toured three ideal spots for fundraising (the feed store, the casino, and the local salon), and even took a

---

[4] Nevarez, Poncho. "Interview with State Representative Poncho Nevarez." Personal interview. 10 Jan. 2017.

web based approach to campaigning by creating the "Opie for Mayor 2013" Facebook page in order to organize his campaign and post objectively amusing content.

Opie went onto raise around $2000 and won the election for mayor! Opie's owner told the LA Times that the losers in the race were "not happy" about the election results, but like the results or not, Opie became the presiding mayor of Anza.

However, the LA Times reported that Opie's reign as the mayor of Anza was met with some challenges. A few residents in Anza began to fear that people would not take the town seriously because of Opie, and that his position may hurt local business. These same residents decided that Opie had to go, and tried to oust him from office –but they were met with a lot of pushback by other residents in Anza. One of Opie's supporters, Nancy Ross, revealed the basis by which support for Opie was made reasonable in her mind by stating "Opie stood for the reason that so many people moved out here" and "we don't want some human sitting on a throne".

The big question here is "how could a person be outdone by a goat?" To rule out the option of "the people of Lajitas just really want goats to hold all public offices", we spoke to Poncho Nevarez, the

Texas State Representative whose district encompasses Lajitas, to get a better grasp of the electorate. During our interview, State Rep. Nevarez described the people in and around Lajitas as "a fiercely independent group who have found a great way to send a message to their local government. Clay Henry was both a nod to the community's ability to self-deprecate and a poke in the eye to the government. Their decision to elect Clay Henry ended up revitalizing Lajitas with a stream of tourists, and for that the Lajitas community has only themselves to thank."

As far as what led them to vote for Clay Henry, State Rep. Nevarez shares with us the belief that it was a lack of connection with voters and a failure to identify that they wanted something other than the status quo. After watching the election of Donald Trump we have all experienced an election that was in part a reaction to the status quo, but it has certainly happened before.

That One Time Minnesota Elected a WWF Wrestler to Governor

"People in Washington were as surprised as if Fidel Castro came looping through on a hippopotamus."

-Dan Rather on the election of Jesse Ventura[5]

"We shocked the world," said Jesse Ventura in his victory speech after winning the governor's office in Minnesota.[6] Three people ran for the governorship. One of the first candidates was Democrat Hubert H. Humphrey III, the current attorney general of the state and son of a long time senator, former vice president, and Democratic nominee for President.[7] The second person was Republican Norm Coleman, the current mayor of Saint Paul, the second biggest city in Minnesota. The final person ran a campaign that Hillary Clinton would go onto describe as a "carnival sideshow" – former WWF wrestler Jesse Ventura, running as a Reform candidate.[8]

---

[5] http://www.mrc.org/bozells-column/remembering-ratherisms

[6] Ventura, Jesse. "Jesse Ventura Victory Speech." Youtube.com. Web. 3 Jan. 2017.

[7] https://www.leg.state.mn.us/legdb/fulldetail?ID=10270

[8] Ventura, Jesse, and Dick Russell. "Thinking Politics

The whole state knew who the Democratic and Republican candidates were, but who exactly was Jesse Ventura? To put it shortly, he was not the usual candidate for governor. A native of Minnesota, Jesse Ventura graduated from high school and joined the US Navy. After being honorably discharged, he joined a motorcycle gang in California. Years later, after returning to Minnesota, a wrestling promoter offered Jesse a job as a wrestler.[9]

He wrestled for 10 years in the WWF, and despite not being the best wrestler, he gained a significant following from his personality onstage. He retired, in part, for medical reasons after discovering that he had a pulmonary embolism, but smoothly transitioned into an announcer job and even starred in a few movies.

In 1990, he made his first political debut when he ran for mayor of Brooklyn Park against an incumbent, and pulled off an upset victory.[10] After

---

in Bush Country." Don't Start the Revolution without Me!: From the Minnesota Governor's Mansion to the Baja Outback: Reflections and Revisionings. New York: Skyhorse Pub., 2008. N. pag. Print.

[9] http://www.biography.com/people/jesse-ventura-9542225

[10] http://www.imdb.com/name/nm0001818/bio

serving as a mayor for a term he went onto host several radio talk shows.

Finally, in 1997, he decided to run for governor as the Reform Party's candidate and brought with him a political agenda that seemed to be a strange combination for the current Minnesota political landscape. Since you already know the punch line of this story, you may be asking yourself "was it really that improbable that he would win?" Going off the opinion of pundits, that answer would be a solid yes.

Not only did Ventura maintain a miserable 10% of the polls for a majority of the race, experts could not wrap their head around how any reasonable person could bring themselves to actually vote for Ventura. (It is also interesting to note that Ventura actually never led in any of the large public polls – even on Election Day). Pundits likely couldn't come to terms with Ventura being a legitimate contender because of his background as a WWF wrestler, his knack for out-of-place comments, and his serious lack of working knowledge about what the governor of Minnesota even does. Here are some notable comments and quotes:

1. "I asked the Dalai Lama the most important question that I think you

could ask – if he had ever seen Caddyshack."[11]

2. "I don't want your stupid money": a direct line from one of his ads that was addressed to special interest groups[12]

3. In an interview with Playboy, he said organized religion "was a sham and a crutch for weak minded people."[13]

4. He openly regarded underwear as superfluous.[14]

5. As the governor, he had no idea that he had to appoint some judges (pretty big thing to overlook).

6. One of Ventura's more popular campaign shirts said "my governor can beat up your governor".

7. Finally, in the 1987 Predator film, Ventura offers people in his squadron chewing tobacco and when he is denied says "This stuff will make you a goddamned sexual Tyrannosaurus, just like me!"[15]

---

[11] http://abcnews.go.com/Politics/story?id=121685

[12] Lentz, Jacob. "The Advertisements." Electing Jesse Ventura: A Third-party Success Story. Boulder: Lynne Rienner, 2002. N. pag. Print.

[13]http://articles.latimes.com/2002/jun/19/nation/na-ventura19/2

[14]http://articles.chicagotribune.com/2010-12-12/news/ct-met-10-things-underwear_1_underwear-undergarment-bra

So there was no doubt that what pundits were thinking of Jesse Ventura was definitely not unfounded. Despite it all, Ventura began to climb from his stagnant 10% position in September, and slowly but surely rose in the polls all the way till Election Day.

Ventura began to catch up because he tapped into a different set of voters than past Minnesota gubernatorial elections have relied on. In the minds of the politically astute, there was a belief that a reasonable voter would choose either Coleman (the Saint Paul Mayor) or Hubert (the Attorney General), but what they were about to find out was that a lot reasonable voters would decide on Ventura based on his message of defying business as usual.

The 1998 Minnesota governor's race had record breaking participation, due in large part to an unprecedented amount of young men and first time voters.[16] It seems as though the average voter in Minnesota did not really care about Ventura's past, and was more focused on the fact that he was not part of the establishment. An LA Times article stated that even though 41% of people polled by the St. Paul

---

[15] Ventura, Jesse. "Predator." *Youtube.com*. Web. 4 Jan. 2017.

[16]https://polmeth.wustl.edu/files/polmeth/lacy00b.pdf

Pioneer Press considered Ventura "an embarrassment to the state" after the election, 59% people agreed that he was a "breath of fresh air" in the same poll.

So in this particular example, pundits, political experts, and the opposition candidates themselves failed to see Jesse Ventura as a feasible candidate because they were sure that almost no one would vote for a former wrestler with a knack for saying wacky things with barely any political experience. However, it turns out that the strongest asset Ventura brought to the table was his lack of his political experience – and it was so strong that it essentially won him the election. Outside of just helplessly watching as Ventura climbed the polls, what could his opponents have done to stop Ventura?

We believe that Coleman and Hubert both lacked a good grasp on what the electorate really wanted. They may have known how they were doing in relation to him in polls they would conduct periodically, but had they taken the investment to find out what Ventura's real draw was they could have had a fighting chance against him. They could have pushed the argument that he was really part of the establishment and they were not, which may have swayed an important margin of voters.

As time has passed data has become increasingly important and not having enough of it or the right kind of it can lead to a quick defeat. This even holds true in elections much smaller than a governor's race.

The Data Lighthouse

You are the captain of a new ship, and you're fighting some of the worst fog you have ever seen. In the distance you can hear the sounds of waves crashing against the shore, but you cannot see which part of the shore is safe harbor and which part will smash your ship to bits. You are now relying solely on the faint sounds that you can hear and your intuition to guide your ship. In an election, if you are running on what you or a small group of people think is important to the voters without any data, you are sailing blindly into a foggy shore. There is a chance you make it, but there is a much larger chance that you smash your ship into the rocks (lose the election). In this scenario, data is analogous to a lighthouse in that it provides you a guideline to safe harbor. Moving away from hypotheticals, we actually were able to experience an election that performed without much data, and much like the probable fate of a ship sailing blindly into a foggy shore, it was battered against the rocks.

Some years ago my brother and I found ourselves sitting in the living room of a successful business owner who had recently decided to run for a big state position. We had been recruited into the campaign by friends and decided we would volunteer our time and efforts to the candidate's campaign.

Upon entering a strategic planning meeting of the campaign, we were introduced to the political consultants running the campaign, two well-dressed and intelligent individuals with a winning track record in prior campaigns throughout the community. The consultants outlined their strategy to the rest of the campaign team, explaining what neighborhoods to reach out to and which neighborhoods were predicted to be solidly in our candidate's favor. As the meeting went on, it became apparent that much work was still needed to be done to get the campaign from where it was to where the consultants wanted it to be.

The clearest issue was the difficulty in conveying the message of the campaign to the people, and in identifying what specific campaign messages the people wanted to hear. At this point the messaging and policy platform itself was not fully made. So my brother and I, pulled out our laptops, created a Google doc, and began hammering away a policy platform for the candidate to publicly post on his website. We worked together into the night alongside the candidate considering all sides of all of the largest issues we could think of. We tried our best to ensure the message we put out was a balance of what the candidate believed and what the people wanted.

The trouble was, we didn't have a real way of knowing what the most important issues were to the people, how important those issues really were to them, and where we were underperforming without paying for a political poll. Much of what we went on was intuition and the advice of the political consultants. We felt uncomfortable not relying on data, but we had no choice. The collection of data is expensive, time consuming, and complicated –a task too large for our small campaign at that time. And why take the time to collect and crunch all the data when the campaign could pay consultants to reach the same end? Unfortunately, those political consultants were wrong.

When the results rolled in on Election Day, it quickly became clear, that the issues the consultants mentioned were important were not, and the areas they assured were locked up strongly in support of our candidate were far from a lock. Election Day exposed the flaws of driving a ship to shore without the guidance of a data lighthouse.

Often, we are told what the reasonable voter will do from the media and political consultants, and make predictions based upon these assessments. Their predictions sometimes are founded on what the professionals believe their version of a reasonable voter will want from a candidate. They typically base their assumptions of how a reasonable voter will act based upon their experiences in past elections, and other times base it on pure intuition. The political consultants would throw around statements like "the people in this town want this" and "the people in the town over there want that", but we really had no idea if what they were saying was true or current. These statements are at their core flawed because they are based on the political consultants' personal reasonable voter paradigm, which did not correctly factor in the unique features that lead voters to make a reasonable decision.

During this campaign, my brother and I saw firsthand how fatal the reliance on the intuition of consultants can be as opposed to using data to guide your decisions. In fact, sometimes those consultants are smash-this-ship-into-the-rocks wrong. The next question is, what is the ideal way to collect data?

Most Complete Way to Fill Out an Incomplete Voter Profile

Early Saturday mornings for kids are usually reserved for cartoons, but not during election season for my siblings and I. Our mom was the campaign manager for our local school board race and Saturdays during election season meant that everyone who was able bodied was out block-walking. Many people have a stereotype of campaign managers as neurotic people who are always on their phone and have horrible family lives. Fortunately, this stereotype did not hold for our mom.

Collected, thorough, and mindful - to both her job and family - are the three words that best describe our mom as a campaign manager. She never brought her work home and yet still somehow managed to drop all of us off at school and pick us up at the end of the day. On the job, however, she was unmatched. To date, she has never lost a campaign that she managed, and since she is now retired from campaigns and a professor at a local college, it seems her record will remain perfect in perpetuity.

The area of a school board race is typically smaller than the area for a mayoral election, making it feasible to gather information in the most complete way possible. This is because, the most complete way to gather information is to get to every voter in your district by knocking on each individual door and asking what issues matter to them and their opinions. Our mom defined thoroughness in her data collection. She would comb through whole neighborhoods with groups of volunteers, marking houses when no one was home in order to return to later in the day. In the instances she could not drum up enough volunteers, she used paid staff. While this would make block-walking a significant expense in those campaigns, our mom would have it no other way. Competing campaigns spent lavish amounts on large fancy signs for every street corner. But as our mom has always said, "signs don't vote."

As a campaign manager our mom discovered that, on almost every issue, opposing school board candidates shared the same view. What separated them were the issues they focused on during the campaign. So she refined her candidate's talking points using the data gathered.

However, her thorough block-walking approach is hard, time devouring, and costly to apply in a race larger than school board elections. Therefore, unless well funded, a fledgling campaign likely cannot afford to collect information this way. But there is a larger problem with this type of polling.

What if, after you spend the money for an exhaustive block-walking poll, the public changes its mind?

Dynamic Reasoning: Plan on it

I still remember sitting in the living room with my brother listening to a new politician ignite a crowd when he excitedly yelled his tagline "Yes We Can". This was of course during the 2008 presidential election, and soon to be President Barack Obama had an incredible message of hope and optimism for the people of the United States in a time when the country's future seemed bleak. Barack Obama ran on a platform of change and hope for a better tomorrow. He of course also had a lot of policy ideas that gave his message some weight. On that message, millions of people across the country voted for him, but one state in particular we would like to focus on is Michigan (and not because my brother and I are massive Detroit Lions fans).

In Michigan, millions of people voted for Obama, and those same people openly cheered when he won. They partied in the streets and were as happy as any Obama supporter was across the country. However, eight years later the state of Michigan experienced an incredible shift. Michigan went from aligning with what Obama was pitching in 2008 and 2012 to moving far across the aisle and helping to elect Donald Trump to the presidency.

A number of the same people who voted for

Barack Obama, and even applauded his victory, would get behind the curtain of a voting booth and vote for Donald Trump.[17] One would imagine that once a state goes one way for two straight elections it would be very hard to flip. Hillary Clinton came off to many as a continuation of the Barack Obama's presidency, which is what people wanted four years ago and four years before that. Donald Trump ran on a number of points, and going into those points in nuance would be beyond the scope of this book, but let's just acknowledge that were very different from Hillary and Barack's agenda. So how could a swing like this happen?

The answer is simple but critical; voters have dynamic reasoning behind their decisions. What brings people out to the polls one year may not bring them to the polls the next year. What voters think is a big issue today, may not even be in their top five most important issues a couple of days after a big news story breaks.

This is one of the major flaws in the ideal way to poll that was outlined in the chapter before this one. Sure going from door to door across the country is the most thorough way to discover how a certain issue is viewed, but what happens when a

---

[17] http://time.com/voices-from-democratic-counties-where-trump-won-big/

circumstance of that issue changes? Well your whole poll could be useless if that circumstance mattered enough. This seems obvious, but this is a problem that my brother and I have seen a lot of smaller campaigns suffer through. Small campaigns, in particular, tend to rely heavily on word of mouth and the advice of political consultants to decide which issues the public is asking to be addressed.

Put yourself in the shoes of a candidate who is running for school board in a small district in South Texas. You have a good feel on the pulse of the community, and you have decided after enough feedback in the form of informal polls and advice from political consultants that the issues to focus on are teacher's pay and new textbooks for the local elementary. Then three weeks from the election a story breaks out. A teacher in your district has been charged with sexual assault, and it has been found that the teacher had a previous history of sexual misconduct before they were hired. What do you do? Should you stick with the issues that you believe were going to win you the election or do you switch and address this topic?

Clearly in this situation you need to address the sexual harassment charge because of how heinous the nature of the crime is, but there are a number of issues where what to do is not entirely clear.

For instance, imagine you are in the same type of situation, but instead of sexual harassment, the teacher was busted for a DWI charge and it happened on campus. Now things are going to get a little murky. You would ideally like to stick with the issues that are important to the community, yourself, and that you felt were likely to win you the position. A DWI charge is not usually heinous enough to make the news, so it is unclear that this charge is known to the people outside the rumor mill. However, you have no idea how far that mill goes. You also have no gauge on how much voters would like to focus on this issue, and that is the problem with going door to door polling. One event could throw the whole poll out the window, and that poll likely cost you a significant amount of money.

We feel like bigger campaigns have the money to poll more consistently (weekly basis or so) so they aren't incredibly impacted, but even this edge is falling as news is coming at us at an ever increasing speed. Because they have very few cost effective options available to them, small campaigns get absolutely devastated by these swings. Fortunately, there have been new polling methods developed to address this issue for both big and small campaigns.

"The Babe Ruth of Polling" (or the "Barry Sanders of Polling")

In 1932 a young editor of the Daily Iowan, a local newspaper, by the name of George Gallup had developed a method of measuring who actually was read the paper. In implementing this method Gallup had an idea, what if he could apply his method to predict political elections?[18] This young pollster was convinced that polls on toothpaste and politics were one in the same. Gallup believed that understanding what people like and how they will act was nothing more than a numbers game—and to him the way polls were being conducted were just wrong. Before the first Gallup poll, the main outlet for polling was the famed Literary Digest, and Gallup believed the Digest predictions of the presidential election of 1936 were going to be a disaster. So, George conducted his own poll based on his own method, Gallup's first poll geared towards an election. In doing so Gallup hoped to show how much better his poll would do in comparison to the Literary Digest. His poll predicted Franklin D. Roosevelt would win the presidential election while the Digest predicted the opponent Alfred M. Landon would win. George's poll predicted both a Roosevelt victory and even how much the Digest poll would be wrong by (predicting

---

[18] http://time.com/4568359/george-gallup-polling-history/

they would pick Landon by 56%). On election night Gallup's predictions were right, Roosevelt had won and he had accurately predicted the Digest's call within 1%. In doing so, Gallup started something that would significantly change the history of American politics. Polling would become a cornerstone of American politics that all campaigns would rely on for guidance on issues for decades.

Election polling has evolved considerably since Gallup's first election poll. Polls went from postcards to telephones, and now we see internet surveys. We also now see polls presented to the public in new ways, either published on various blogs or by entrepreneurial pollsters such as Nate Silver of FiveThirtyEight. These new ways of presenting polling are far removed from the traditional media— the former gatekeepers of reliable polling data. Polling is now a field filled with personalities who reign as kings at times. Like all kingdoms, no reign lasts forever, and any king can fall quickly.

The death of the Literary Digest is associated with the failed predictions in the presidential election of 1936 leading to the rise of George Gallup.[19] More recently, John Zogby, a pollster once dubbed the "Prince of pollsters" for his work in the 90's and early

[19]https://sites.duke.edu/hillygus/files/2014/06/Hillygus POQpolling.pdf

2000's was eventually dragged through the mud after numerous incorrect predictions. At one point Zogby was criticized by the newest king Nate Silver, who called him, "The Worst Pollster in the World."[20] Ironically even more recently, Nate Silver himself may see his reputation as a "guru" wiped away after his failed prediction of the 2016 presidential election. One headline after the election, "Nate Silver Blew it Bigly on the Election" after Silver had predicted that Clinton had a 71.4% chance of winning the presidential election on the morning of the election. Today, Nate Silver is the pollster closest to having the trust that George Gallup had back in 1948, but Silver and his fellow pollsters have hit a recent streak of incorrect predictions, leading the faith in the entire field to erode. The most recent failed predictions of massive elections like Britain's "Brexit" referendum and United States presidential election of 2016 have led many to ask, why have the pollsters been getting election predictions so wrong?

Despite being horribly inaccurate at times, polling remains the best known way to predict an election. They still provide data on critical information to ensure a campaign has a lighthouse to prevent it from crashing into the rocks, but recently their reliability has become questionable. We believe

---

[20] http://fivethirtyeight.com/features/worst-pollster-in-world-strikes-again/

the reason these polls have incorrectly predicted past elections is because they are failing to find a way to account for the innovation factor in campaigns. The innovation factor often appears as a campaign capitalizing on new tools and or messaging opportunities, and there are few better examples of this than the election of Barack Obama.

"Yes We Can"

Late one evening in the fall of 2007, my brother and I avoided our homework, and sat around our living room table glued to our TV. That day we, like millions of other millennials, were inspired by a passionate and hope inspiring speech delivered by the most articulate politician we had ever been confronted with—Barack Obama. But on that day, the rest of the country wasn't exactly as inspired with then Senator Obama. Barack Obama was polling almost 30 points below his primary opponent Hillary Clinton, a difference people believed was too large to overcome.[21][22] Many pundits began discussing what it would be like to have a primary where Clinton had no opponents by the time the campaign got to New Hampshire—because opponents like Obama were predicted to drop out of the race.

The pundits' predictions and the low polls were no surprise. Obama was a young politician with two years of national political experience as the junior Senator from Illinois and eight years as a state Senator. Unlike other candidates that had succeeded at young ages such as John F. Kennedy, Obama did

---

[21] http://www.realclearpolitics.com/epolls/2008/preside nt/us/democratic_presidential_nomination-191.html

[22] http://thecaucus.blogs.nytimes.com/2007/10/19/prima ry-decisions-for-december/

not hail from a politically successful family, he was not wealthy, and he was not the favorite of the political establishment. While Obama was charismatic, charming, and ambitious his resume was not comparable to Hillary Clinton. To use a college basketball analogy, even if Barack Obama was a March Madness Cinderella story that runs the table, getting as far as the Final Four, Hillary Clinton was still the perennial powerhouse that eventually ends the dream and takes the national championship.

Hillary's campaign on the other hand was one with all of the right tools and features that successful campaigns in the past had, making Hillary's campaign seemingly destined to succeed. Hillary was a well-known national figure, a Senator from New York for seven years, and, a First Lady that tackled more policy work than the norm for a First Lady. Her campaign was one many saw coming, it was meticulously planned, extraordinarily well funded, and one many powerful people within D.C. clearly supported.

While Obama was unknown, Hillary had been under the national spotlight for over a decade. Obama had less money, while Hillary had the majority of the Democratic establishment behind her. Obama was young and still relatively inexperienced. How could someone like him win such an uphill battle?

Iowa

"You know, they said this day would never come. They said our sights were set too high...But on this January night, at this defining moment in history, you have done what the cynics said we couldn't do."

-Barack Obama

Despite so many features and indicators pointing towards a loss for Barack Obama, his campaign managed to do what the Washington insiders said was impossible, he upset Hillary Clinton, the establishment candidate with everything going for her. On January 3, 2008 Obama won the first primary contest between him and Clinton, and as you know he became the Democratic nominee and defeated John McCain, to become the 44th President of the United States.

How did he upset such a well-established candidate? Many say that he was able to tap into something within the people, that he represented the change the people wanted, or that Hillary Clinton herself could not compete with him. However, there was more to Obama's upset than impassioned supporters on TV, more than charisma, and more than inspiring people with his message of hope and change. The Obama campaign was the most tech savvy campaign the United States had ever seen. Underneath the hood of the Obama campaign was an engine of innovation, willingness to use tech, and new methods of organization that powered one of the most memorable campaigns in modern history. Obama put innovation and tech at the forefront of his campaign by recruiting innovators like 24-year old Chris Hughes, cofounder of Facebook, to work as the director of internal organizing and to help them develop technology never before used in American politics.

MyBO

The Obama campaign went onto recruit and hire many other innovators like Hughes. These innovators worked with the Obama campaign to develop an online networking tool dubbed, "MyBO" (we think they could have thought of a better name) to power what would become a new era of campaign organizing and networking of supporters.[23] MyBO played a significant role in the campaign's overall success, particularly in caucus states.

On March 4th 2008, also known as "Super Tuesday" I was caught up in other matters regarding the 2008 primaries, this time it was not to watch the coverage of the 2008 primaries, but to participate in the primary. However I did not participate by voting per se, I was participating the Texas way, by diving into the "Texas Two-Step." You see, in Texas during the 2008 primary, a voter could participate in two ways, they could vote at the poles and then if a voter chose, they could then choose again at a caucus in their district after the polls closed.[24] So on that night my brother and I were taken by our Mom, who at that time was a strong Clinton supporter, over to an old

[23]https://people.stanford.edu/jaaker/sites/default/files/te brmay-june-obama.pdf
[24]https://www.texastribune.org/2015/07/07/texplainer-whats-texas-two-step-and-why-it-gone/

school gym down the street from our house. At that gym we witnessed firsthand the strength and reach that technology could have on a campaign—we watched Obama supporters organized with MyBO defeat Clinton supporters in a precinct with a majority of Clinton supporters. With MyBO the Obama campaign was able to deliver marching orders to every Texan registered with MyBO. MyBO was able to develop lists of volunteers by geographic micro-regions and pair people with appropriate tasks, including preparing nearby voters on caucus procedure. That night the Obama supporters in the gym were prepared, well educated, and organized—all as a result of the new tech tool that seemed to function as a secret weapon more than anything. Obama won the caucus in the gym that night, as well as the overall caucus votes in Texas, 99 to 94.[25]

---

[25] https://www.technologyreview.com/s/410644/how-obama-really-did-it/

A/B Testing

Early in the primary campaign, Senator Obama went to Mountain View to give a talk at Google that a man by the name of Dan Siroker attended. At this talk, Siroker was so inspired by Obama that he decided to take a leave of absence from his job at Google to do what he could to assist the Obama campaign. Siroker's decision eventually led to the birth of a company named Optimizely. Optimizely was created after the Obama campaign in '08, born from an innovative technique—A/B testing. In 2008, A/B testing was a cutting edge technique. A/B testing is a method of comparing a few variations of advertisements, mainly web pages and web designs, to find which page is better—with the goal of making the most compelling web pages and ads. Simply put, A/B testing is a method of finding out how to best attract someone's attention, converting what was previously an art into more of a science. To further explain, A/B testing is done by comparing the original version of one page (page A) with a variation of that page (page B), and then the one that performs better in its ability to get more "signup" or "donate" clicks wins the challenge, simple right? It's a data driven method of finding the best way to get volunteers, donations, and social shares (Facebook, Twitter, Instagram). This simple method of making the best ads was something campaigns had never seen before until Dan Siroker joined the Obama campaign.

When Siroker arrived the "new media" team was attempting make the site better at getting volunteers and donations, so Siroker applied A/B to rethink the entire layout of the campaign website. Under Siroker's watch the campaign was able to find that small things like word choice could yield significant increases in clicks and overall signups. Using A/B testing the campaign was able to see that the combination of images like a picture of Obama's family with a "Learn More" button increased signups by 40 percent.[26] What was truly amazing though, was how wrong members of the campaign were when they approached web design as an art.

---

[26] https://www.wired.com/2012/04/ff_abtesting/

CONTROL	WITH IMAGE

↑ +6.9%

http://kylerush.net

CONTROL	"SEQUENTIAL"

↑ +5%

At one point, almost every staffer believed that a video would fare much better at getting signups than a still image—in reality the video did 30.3 percent worse than an image. Instincts would have accidently led the staffers down a path of making a lower quality web page. By the end of the campaign, very careful estimates showed that 4 million of the 13 million addresses in the campaign's email list were the direct result of Siroker's A/B testing. And perhaps the most jaw dropping thing, the emails and additional signups amounted to a significant spike in overall donations—as much as $60 million.[27]

Tech innovations and new techniques such as MyBO and A/B testing were what secretly powered the unlikely upset for the Obama campaign back in 2008. The success of the innovations were not lost on the campaign staffers, many of whom took the technology they developed and created their own startups.

In fact, the Obama campaign, in many ways served as the incubator for many startups, appropriately dubbed the, "Obama start-ups" that were spun off into many successful private companies.[28] To name one, Optimizely now uses its capabilities to serve more than just political campaigns it now delivers cutting edge marketing experiences via their experimentations platform.[29]

---

[27] https://blog.optimizely.com/2010/11/29/how-obama-raised-60-million-by-running-a-simple-experiment/

[28] http://www.economist.com/news/business/21567403-techniques-presidents-election-campaigns-have-spawned-one-lot-young-firms-obama

Even after an incredible amount of political innovations were fostered by the Obama campaign, we begin to see the wheels of innovation turn once again during the Bernie Sanders campaign.

---

[29] http://www.businessinsider.com/optimizely-raises-58-million-2015-10

Big Organizing

2016 was no stranger to political innovations; many of those innovations came from the Bernie Sanders campaign, which revolutionized the political arena (despite not succeeding over Hillary Clinton).

In the early summer of 2015 I received a Facebook message from my brother that contained a video about an Independent Senator from Vermont that had decided to run against Hillary Clinton for President in the Democratic primary—Bernie Sanders. This video was unlike other campaign videos, which would usually just outline the candidate and their past accomplishments. This video showed one of Bernie Sanders' rallies that had taken the nation by storm. Bernie was filling convention centers and stadiums from New Hampshire to Seattle, even packing a massive crowd in Houston, which was remarkable to watch. I recall thinking, "I haven't read much about this guy, but maybe I should start." The Sanders campaign had a strong understanding of their supporters and Bernie's message resonated deeply with those he reached out to. The Sanders campaign (or better said, the Sanders movement) had a unique feature to it, it seemed to come of out nowhere with momentum that literally grew at an exponential rate. Being a product of passion rather than a well funded and well organized campaign, the momentum of support outpaced the growth of the campaign itself, creating a problem—the campaign needed a way to organize all its support.

For those that followed the 2016 election, the Sanders campaign was one of the biggest stories, because of the passion and fanatical following of the Sanders supporters, which Sanders supporters dubbed the "political revolution". Their energy was a kind the country had not seen since 2008 during the Obama campaign, an energy willing and able to turn a relatively unknown "Independent" U.S Senator from Vermont into a household name who launched a very serious and nearly successful bid for President of the United States. The funny thing about his campaign though, like I mentioned, was that it ran on momentum as opposed to traditional campaigns which are usually led by veteran political consultants. The "political revolution" was a wave of momentum the official Sanders campaign staff could not have manufactured if it had ten times the funding and experience. What distinguished this campaign and waive of momentum from other populist campaigns with similar potential was how the passionate supporters making up the "political revolution" organized themselves.[30] The supporters themselves organized and directed their efforts in a way that harnessed innovation and tech, leveraging passionate supporters into a presidential campaign the country had to pay attention to.[31] Organizing on platforms such as Reddit and Slack, the supporters were able to gather in one virtual location and then very effectively dole out duties and responsibilities in a manner that was truly unprecedented.[32] If the 2012 presidential campaign was about "Big Data," the 2015-2016 Sanders campaign was in many ways driven by "Big Organizing."[33]

[30] https://www.thenation.com/article/how-the-sanders-campaign-is-reinventing-the-use-of-tech-in-politics/

[31] http://www.politico.com/magazine/story/2016/02/bernie-sanders-army-of-coders-2016-213647

[32] https://www.nytimes.com/2015/09/04/us/politics/bernie-sanders-presidential-campaign-tech-supporters.html

Fielding the Bern

In January of 2016 thousands of enthusiastic volunteers walked the streets of Des Moines, Iowa, "pounding pavement" block by block to spread the message about Bernie Sanders. Unpaid volunteers in campaigns are nothing new, but the Sanders campaign was able to add an extra wrinkle unique to their campaign—efficient onboarding of their volunteers. The Sanders campaign had no shortage of support from passionate people, which was clear from the massive rallies he would hold across the country. However what was remarkable was how the Sanders campaign was able to transfer the passion and support into organized action. With innovative tech created by Sanders supporters, the supporters themselves made a way to efficiently direct and transfer their passion into action by automating the onboarding process of volunteers.

Before if you were interested in volunteering and working on a political campaign you would need to make contact with the campaign, formally signup, meet an individual within the campaign, go through a training with a campaign staff member, receive the appropriate campaign information such as lists of potential voters and flyers, and then maybe you

---

[33] http://www.bernkit.com/#f=All

would be set to volunteer your valuable time to a campaign. But with this innovation, much of that was automated. The Field the Bern app streamlined the process that could have taken as long as a week to occur, into a matter of seconds.[34] This allowed interested volunteers to download the app, log in, then begin impacting the election in their local communities. While there is much to say about this brilliant app, one of the most amazing details about it had nothing to do with the software. The creators— passionate Sanders supporters, were not even directly affiliated with the Sanders campaign itself. The app was a perfect matching of tech with the old school election practice of block-walking, making the Sanders campaign far more efficient as well as giving the campaign a way to positively take advantage of its supporter's energy.

---

[34] https://www.wired.com/2016/01/sanders-new-canvassing-app-on-boards-volunteers-in-seconds/

Using the app, volunteers were able to get access to information on how to canvas, such as sample scripts directing them on what to say and information on Bernie Sanders, including his platform.[35] This was significant because most campaigns provide this information via training (taking the time of paid staff members) or printed packets (increasing costs and reducing efficiency). The app also gave volunteers the ability to see which homes and places other volunteers had already been to while freely allowing each volunteer the ability to visit any home they chose—and track their progress along the way. The app even gamified the volunteer

[35] http://time.com/4168802/bernie-sanders-canvassing-app/

block-walking process, giving them five points for every door they knocked on and ten points for every piece of information they updated, so they could see how they ranked against other volunteers.

Through this innovation, created by volunteers of the campaign itself, the Sanders campaign was able to convert passion and energy from yelling, sign holding, and political Facebook posting into organized and targeted block-walking. We have observed that organized block-walking is critical to the success of a campaign because the contact of a volunteer—a real human—at your doorstep telling you why you should support a candidate is significantly more persuasive than yard signs. As our Mom used to always say, "signs don't vote", voters need to be convinced not only who to vote for, but to get out and vote in general. And when it comes to getting people off of their couches and into a voting booth, few things are as effective as real human contact with another informed and passionate person explaining why they are so passionate. However, when you can't get on someone's doorstep, sometimes a text message may be the next best thing.

"Why call when you can text?"

During the winter of 2016 many Bernie Sanders supporters received text messages directly from Sanders volunteers.[36] While this seems simple, this was not a run of the mill campaign strategy. Most volunteers are assigned the task of calling supporters directly. Once a volunteer is onboarded and trained, they typically are provided a call sheet and directed to call every person on the list. Now, the difference between a phone call and text seem slight, but the impact is significant, especially to young people.[37]

In 2017 a lot of us can appreciate the difference between communicating via text message and calling, especially with a stranger. How many of us opt to flatly ignore a call from an unknown number? But how many of us would consider responding to a text message sent from an actual person? At the very least we are much more likely to read the contents of a text sent directly to our phone. Especially when the text explains who the sender is, how they got your number, and asks a question that begs a simple response. Even better, what if a campaign could use a tool that allowed volunteers to

---

[36] http://www.dailydot.com/layer8/hustle-app-bernie-sanders-texting/

[37] http://www.gallup.com/poll/179288/new-era-communication-americans.aspx

manage hundreds of text conversations at the same time? This simple text messaging strategy was made a reality and effectively implemented by the Sanders campaign by an app named, "Hustle."[38]

> *"Hey <lead name>! This is John Doe an organizer for the Bernie campaign in Germantown. I'm going to be at Starbucks all day Monday and would love to talk to you about how you can help us win Maryland. When are you free?"*

---

[38]http://www.recode.net/2016/5/2/11634146/bernie-sanders-organizing-app

In the midst of the Democratic primaries between Sanders and Clinton a field organizer for Sanders, Zach Fang, stumbled on the realization that the connecting power of text messaging could be harnessed and leveraged by technology.[39] Before the

---

[39] http://www.dailydot.com/layer8/hustle-app-bernie-sanders-texting/

Iowa caucuses Fang attempted to use an app that at its core was a "peer-to-peer" messaging app made to let users/volunteers handle a huge number of text conversations. Fang could not have predicted the resulting impact his idea would have. Fang realized that with an app like Hustle a volunteer could send 800 messages per hour, a huge difference from phone banking where a volunteer could likely not make over 50 phone calls in an hour. And what was really amazing was that the response rate of a text message was over 3 times higher than a phone call at first.

This was a monumental difference, with Hustle the Sanders campaign pioneered a tool that most if not all campaigns moving forward will likely use. A tool that allows the work of a volunteer to be more efficient by amplifying the amount of human connections a volunteer can make. With Hustle, and other tools like it, the ability for a handful of volunteers to do the work of scores of phone bankers may soon be a reality.

At one point in the Sanders campaign, a single volunteer with Hustle proved to be 17 times more effective than phone banking volunteers in getting confirmations to an important campaign dinner.[40] The phone bankers made 23,076 calls in 461 hours—resulting in 465 confirms, while at the same time one

---

[40] https://docsend.com/view/2gd3597

staffer using Hustle got 285 confirms in 16 hours. Hustle essentially gave a campaign volunteer the same amount of influence as a lengthy row of phone bankers working tirelessly.

Innovations like Hustle are disrupting the current state of democratic elections, transforming some of the ways campaigns operate and compete with each other, and often times these innovations can lead to stunning upsets.

#ReachingVoters2016

Right before I walked into work on November 8th I was looking through a FiveThirtyEight article that popped up on my Facebook newsfeed. It had Hillary Clinton with over 70% odds of winning the election. Thinking this election was more or less in the bag I did not check those odds until I showed up at the Texas Democratic Party's Watch Party being held at a hotel in downtown Austin.

Once I got there, I met with friends and secured a spot with a direct line of sight to the news stations delivering live reporting of the results. However, as the night went on Hillary's chances of victory became bleaker and bleaker. I was truly shocked, as soon as the Florida results were reported I got a call from my little brother and we knew it was over. He described the scene at Harvard Law School as people realized that Hillary was going to lose. Sam said, "You can feel the despair here. Not even kidding, the school looks like Hogwarts after Voldemort took over." As he said this I could see Trump supporters in the street celebrating with each other in their trademark "Make America Great Again" hats. I was stunned, and I imagine those at Hillary's headquarters in Brooklyn, with all of their cutting edge data analytics, were shell-shocked as well.

Everybody was wondering "How did this happen?"

As we have mentioned, innovating will help push you towards victory, but the electorate is a fickle beast, and the advantage is often short lived. While many point towards data driven campaign tactics as the secret weapon of Barack Obama's 2012 reelection campaign, doubling down on Barack Obama's approach did not lead to continued victory. As pundits framed the 2016 presidential election, Hillary Clinton's campaign in comparison to Donald Trump's was like a large tanker versus a band of many smaller pirate ships. A comparison which turned out in many respects to be true. As one writer for the Economist put it, "a massive data battleship lost to a chaotic flotilla of social-media speedboats."[41]

While Trump insulted data driven campaign tactics such as those used in Obama's 2012 campaign, he did not completely write off the targeted outreach, he merely altered the way voter outreach was done once they had the data. Trump broke from the tradition of hiring old hands that are campaign veterans, and had his son-in-law Jared Kushner, a

---

[41] https://www.economist.com/news/united-states/21710614-fake-news-big-data-post-mortem-under-way-role-technology

man with no prior campaign experience, to lead the development of a digital outreach strategy.

Kushner enlisted the assistance of a data firm, Cambridge Analytica, whose parent company played a role in assisting the outcome of the "Brexit" vote, another election with a very surprising result.[42] The digital strategy developed was one a presidential campaign had never taken before. According to Matt Oczkowski, the head of the data science team for the Trump campaign at Cambridge Analytica, the Trump campaign applied an almost surgical level of detail only available within online platforms such as Facebook, Pandora, and Snapchat.

To get to voters in the most impactful way, Trump's campaign reached out to them online with a simple strategy; throw out a lot of content, see what works, and scale from there. This new and innovative way of digital outreach should not be confused with Trump's outlandish and sometimes plainly false tweets.

The messages Trump's digital market campaign was sending took the form of online ads such as promoted Facebook posts. Once the campaign found out what stuck with a specific voter they kept

---

[42] https://phys.org/news/2016-12-big-trump-scorned.html

bombarding the voter with that message. However, the Trump campaign was not throwing just anything out there.

The campaign's strategy involved thousands of variations of messages that targeted certain voter profiles on social media platforms like Facebook and Snapchat. By using psychometrics, Cambridge Analytica was able to identify which specific people to target with a specific message by accessing points of data on people. Psychometrics is a scientific field that in short, is a method of better understanding a person. As it turns out, once you have enough information (or data points) on a person, you can understand an incredible amount about someone.[43]

Until 2016, many campaigns had used demographic data in combination with voter history to make assessments on a voter. Alexander Nix, the CEO of Cambridge Analytica argues that doing so is ridiculous. Cambridge Analytica operated on the premise that it was ridiculous for all women to receive the same message because of their gender—or for all African Americans to receive similar messages because of their race.

---

[43] https://motherboard.vice.com/en_us/article/how-our-likes-helped-trump-win

Rather than reach out to a voter based on demographics, Cambridge Analytica chose to reach out to individual people by using their Facebook likes and friends.[44] It turns out, if the Trump campaign reached out to you on Facebook, it was after they understood an immense amount about you, and their marketing to you would reflect that. According to Michal Kosinski, former Deputy Director of the University of Cambridge Psychometrics Centre, the more likes (data points) you have on a person the better you can understand them.[45]

Kosinski's research used a person's Facebook likes to understand them, and he even claimed to be able to evaluate a person better than the average work colleague off of ten Facebook likes.[46] If Kosinski had 70 likes he had enough to understand you as much, if not more, than what a person's friends could, with 150 he could possibly understand them as much as a person's parents did, and with 300 likes he could

---

[44] https://www.youtube.com/watch?v=n8Dd5aVXLCc

[45] *Private traits and attributes are predictable from digital records of human behavior* by M. Kosinski, D. Stillwell, T. Graepel, Proceedings of the National Academy of Sciences (PNAS), 2013. (IF: 9.1).

[46] *Computer-based personality judgments are more accurate than those made by humans* by W. Youyou,* M. Kosinski,* D. Stillwell, Proceedings of the National Academy of Sciences (PNAS), 2015. (*Youyou and Kosinski share the first authorship.) (IF: 9.1),

understand someone as much as the person's partner did about them.

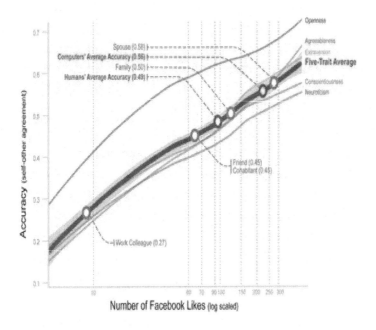

Number of Facebook Likes (log scaled)

Like we mentioned before, it's possible that the Trump campaign knew a whole lot about you before they reached out to you on the internet—and Trump's campaign didn't stop there.

According to Cambridge Analytica, they used almost 4,000 different online ads for Trump, which were viewed 1.5 billion times by millions of Americans during the campaign. These ads were also utilized for fundraising purposes. In a tell all article

Kushner told Forbes that the fundraising for Trump's campaign operated as close to a Silicon Valley startup as possible.

At one point the digital marketing side of the campaign even used machine learning.[47] The campaign's digital marketing hub was installed into a "nondescript" building outside of San Antonio, where a one hundred person team was placed. From San Antonio, the Trump campaign installed digital marketing companies on a trading floor to make them compete for business. Kushner commented that ineffective ads were killed in minutes, while successful ones were scaled.

The campaign sent more than 100,000 uniquely tweaked ads to targeted voters each day. Ultimately, a billionaire running for president, who at one point had his campaign's fundraising effort ridiculed at the beginning of 2016, was able to raise more than $250 million in four months—reportedly from mostly small donors.

No matter what side of the aisle you fall on, there is little dispute that the campaign itself applied incredibly innovative methods and tools. While

---

[47]http://www.forbes.com/sites/stevenbertoni/2016/11/2
2/exclusive-interview-how-jared-kushner-won-trump-the-white-
house/#740dcfcd2f50

technological innovation is often the driver behind upset victories, innovations in ways to effectively deliver your message to the electorate that are not entirely tech based are becoming incredibly important as well.

Humor Wins: *The Tale of the Legendary RotMan Campaign*

In a serious interview, a reporter from the Daily Texan asked Xavier Rotnofsky why he was running to be UT Austin's Student Body President. His response was "to lose weight" followed by Vice President hopeful Rohit Mandalapu answering a question about how qualified they were to run UT Austin's student body by saying "we like to think that we are the least unqualified".[48] Rotnofsky-Mandalapu (lovingly referred to as RotMan) were running a race that many students knew was an uphill battle. As a student at UT Austin during their campaign, it seemed like before RotMan, the candidates that were elected were always the same kind of people. It was a person in a fraternity/sorority or spirit group paired with a similar person that often gave great sounding but inherently weak promises that insisted they were listening to students.

The RotMan campaign was different to say the least. To start, not only were neither of the pair part of a fraternity/sorority or spirit group, they were actually both writers for the Texas Travesty (a

---

[48] Student Government Candidate Profile: Rotnofsky-Mandalapu. Perf. Xavier Rotnofsky & Rohit Mandalapu. The Daily Texan, 3 Mar. 2015. Web. 12 Jan. 2017. <https://www.youtube.com/watch?v=WKv77YLgWUA>.

satirical newspaper similar to The Onion). From the outside, it seemed like since RotMan was not within the political machine, they had very little going for them, but what they did have was a sharp and witty sense of humor.

They posted multiple videos to YouTube featuring jabs at student government like when they describe it as a "group of kids who get together to boost their resumes" or by how they mocked the other candidates by blatantly posting a silhouette of California in their campaign photos instead of Texas. Their platform points included things like "getting a Chilis on campus" and "mandating that student government reps wear cellophane so they are entirely transparent". On request they would Photoshop themselves into pictures of students who were studying abroad, with hilarious results, and even poked fun at the other candidates for proliferating serious profile pictures for their supporters to use by distributing their own with awkward stock photos (picture below).

Rotnofsky
MANDALAPU
What starts here?

Vote March 4th & 5th at
UTEXASVOTE.ORG
For more info visit
www.LetsTalkTexas.biz

Perhaps their greatest stunt will forever be known as LunchablesGate. The pair was invited to participate in a debate with the other student government candidates, and brought their own butler who served the other candidates lunchables and brownies. Rohit Mandalapu even received a haircut on stage while the debate was happening. One of the angry candidates went onto report the RotMan campaign for not including the lunchables in their campaign expenses.[49] The ensuing "scandal" was

[49]http://www.dailytexanonline.com/blogs/the-update/2015/03/12/sg-executive-alliance-candidates-rotnofsky-mandalapu-fined-for-failure

known as LunchablesGate and ended up winning them a lot more support than it lost (talk about your all time backfires). Because they seemingly took nothing serious, a lot of students thought they had no chance to win, but that was all about to change when the first Election Day arrived.

In a huge shock, it was announced that no candidate had won a majority, meaning that there would need to be a runoff between the front-runner campaign and RotMan. The school was stunned, how did they do it? The RotMan campaign had somehow struck a nerve in the student body (who are for the large part of voting age). This is when the genius of their campaign began to show, because everything about their campaign from their constant teasing of student government to the fact that they were unconventional candidates drew out a lot of students who would never vote because of their apathy with student government (myself included). The front-runner campaign (who was very much a pair that would have traditionally won) was beginning to worry, but still few could imagine that RotMan would actually win.

The campaign went onto do things like make a Tinder and Grindr profile in order to talk directly to students in a way that was both hilarious and seemingly very effective. They consistently put out funny content and had amassed thousands of likes on their Facebook page within a few weeks. Then right before the results came out the elections official proudly proclaimed that this had been the largest voter turnout in school history. Finally, she announced that RotMan had done the impossible and beaten out the traditional candidates.

From the RotMan campaign to goats being elected to mayor in Lajitas and Anza, we can clearly see that something about humor has a strong connection with voters. Perhaps it is because humor strikes a good feeling chord in all of us, and when used to criticize the status quo it seems to be easier to process then a gloomy news story. Or maybe it is because of the connection that is established when someone tells you a good joke. If you need more proof of this phenomenon look to the success of satirical news shows like Last Week Tonight with John Oliver or when the Daily Show with Jon Stewart dominated Comedy Central. Both of those shows use comedy to deliver us real news and have become wildly popular.

So clearly when it comes to politics, humor has turned into a new way to reach out to voters, and that is, ironically, no joke.

From Old Push Polling to Modern Fake News

Push Polling

"Would you be more or less likely to vote for Governor Richards if you knew that lesbians dominated her staff?"

-George W. Bush push poll from his 1994 campaign for Texas Governor[50]

In 1994 George W. Bush was running against incumbent Ann Richards for the position of governor. George W. Bush was having a hard time deflecting criticisms that he was just running off his father's name (George H.W. Bush). However, George W. Bush had a tactic up his sleeve that was developed by his father's close political consultant Lee Atwater; push polling.

Push polling is technically not even polling, because there is often no real effort to collect any data. It is mainly just a manipulation technique used by campaigns to push harmful and likely untrue

---

[50] Swansbrough, Robert H. "Challenging an Icon." Test by Fire: The War Presidency of George W. Bush. Basingstoke: Palgrave Macmillan, 2008. N. pag. Print.

rumors about their opponents into the public view under the guise of a legitimate poll.[51] Push polling is seen as a highly unethical of swaying people's opinions, and even its main developer, Lee Atwater, acknowledged this to some extent a short time before his death.

Lee Atwater arrived on the political scene after his work in helping Ronald Reagan win the 1980 Republican nomination.[52] After running Reagan's campaign he was brought in to run George H.W. Bush's 1988 run for president, and this is where his political warfare tactics became famous.

[51]https://www.nytimes.com/2014/06/19/upshot/push-polls-defined.html?_r=0
[52]http://www.nytimes.com/1991/03/30/obituaries/lee-atwater-master-of-tactics-for-bush-and-gop-dies-at-40.html?pagewanted=all

(Lee Atwater)

George H.W. Bush's opponent was former governor of Massachusetts, Michael Dukakis. Lee Atwater's goal was to focus on making Michael Dukakis appear to be an elitist who was out of touch, but ended up doing a lot more than that with his aggressive political attacks. His NY Times Obituary even notes that since Atwater knew that Bush could not win on the issues, he focused on Willie Horton (a black man on a weekend furlough from Massachusetts prison, raped a woman and stabbed her husband) turning him into a central issue of the 1988 election. Atwater was criticized for harnessing racial tensions and for running a campaign that did not focus on macro level issues, and to give you a sense of who Lee Atwater is he responded to similar criticisms concerning George H.W. Bush's presidential campaign by saying "We had only one goal in the campaign: to help elect George Bush. That's the purpose of any political campaign. What other function should a campaign have?"

However, Atwater's brutal campaign methods and in particular, push polling, were born before this race. In a 1980 congressional race Atwater ran a push poll against Tom Turnipseed claiming that at one point "he had been hooked up to jumper cables as a teen undergoing treatment for depression."[53] Despite this accusation being outlandish, it is noted as one of the things that lost Turnipseed the election. (Later Atwater went onto apologize to Turnipseed in a letter for this)

This method continued to be effective especially in George W. Bush's race against Ann Richards in which an infamous Atwater style push poll attempted to sway East Texas voters by asking "Would you be more or less likely to vote for Governor Richards if you knew that lesbians dominated her staff?" This proved to be an effective attack on Ann Richards in East Texas and was one of the factors that contributed to George W. Bush's victory against her. However, now that the Bush family is seemingly done with running campaigns and

[53] https://www.thenation.com/article/lee-atwaters-legacy/

Lee Atwater has passed away, is push polling gone? The short answer is that it has not gone away, it has just evolved.

Back when Lee Atwater developed push polling it was something that the candidates or their team had to orchestrate themselves. This of course leads to the ever present risk that you get caught doing it and publicly shamed. Currently the information that would have normally been distributed by a push poll is now being distributed by strange alternative news sources that make their money off having clickbait type story titles like "5 Pics Obama DOES NOT Want the Public to See." Arguably, this current system may actually be more harmful than the former system of push polling, because as you will read in the coming paragraphs it is totally out of control.

Fake News

If you have been on Facebook recently it is likely that you scrolled by a video of a blonde woman condescendingly screaming conservative points in an incredibly obvious attempt to pander to the right. This woman is named Tomi Lahren, and she actually gets paid to spew out incredibly misleading and sometimes outright false statements on a daily basis.

After Barack Obama gave his farewell address to the nation she released a video that included the following statements commenting on his address[54]:

1. "After the election and reelection of our first black president we don't have much to show for it except for failed Obamacare, failed Iran Deal, failed no strategy for national security, race relations worse now than anytime since the civil rights movement"

2. "The only folks that should be thanking Obama are America's enemies. THEY"VE BEEN THRIVING UNDER OBAMA!" (**we don't think Osama Bin Laden would agree**)

3. Refers to Barack Obama as BO (no trace of love in how she said it) and then says that he "confuses diversity with illegal immigration and ISIS sleeper cell transplants"

You may be thinking, "well that is just one person on an online broadcast, how many people could it possibly reach?" Within 5 days this video had just under 5 million views, and that appears to be the

[54] http://www.theblaze.com/video/tomi-lahren-says-goodbye to barack obama/

case with a large portion of her videos. Honestly, that is 4,999,996 more people than we thought would voluntarily watch her rants (the four being my brother and I watching it for the research and maybe her parents). However, the things Tomi Lahren says are nothing compared to what InfoWars host, Alex Jones, gets away with saying.

We could make up a satirical mission statement for InfoWars, but it still wouldn't be as hilarious as the real one which verbatim reads (it is written in all caps):

"ALEX JONES AND INFOWARS STAND AGAINST THIS ONSLAUGHT. EVERY DAY CONNECTING THE DOTS, PEELING BACK THE ONION. HE DIGS DEEPER INTO THE STORY WITH THE INSIGHT OF EXPERTS, WHISTLEBLOWERS AND INSIDERS. SEEKING THE TRUTH AND EXPOSING THE SCIENTIFICALLY ENGINEERED LIES OF THE GLOBALISTS AND THEIR ULTIMATE GOAL OF ENSLAVING HUMANITY."[55]

Pretty funny, right? We think so too, and his opinions on national and global affairs are pretty much what you would assume they would be. In one of his videos he claims "Ladies and gentleman I can

---

[55] http://www.infowars.com/about-alex-jones/

now report to you that it is true, President Obama is a radical Muslim" and later claims that Obama prays towards Mecca 5 times a day in the White House.[56] Alex Jones seems to be that one strange conspiracy guy who thinks The Matrix was based on fact. Funny enough, he actually did release a report on InfoWars with this title:

"TECH BILLIONAIRES SECRETLY FUNDING SCIENTISTS TO HELP BREAK OUT OF MATRIX REALITY"[57]

The most hilarious part is that he published the above story on October 6th, 2016! Making no attempt to hide his interest of conspiracy theories, unlike a normal person who secretly dabbles in an episode of Ancient Aliens from time to time.

Now here comes the part that is not so funny. Alex Jones, conspiracy theory connoisseur, has been taken seriously by at least one person: Donald Trump. When Donald Trump appeared on the InfoWars Show he told Alex Jones "Your reputation is amazing. I will not let you down."[58] For the country's sake we are all

[56] Secret Service Admit Obama Is A Muslim! Perf. Alex Jones. N.p., 4 Jan. 2016. Web. 7 Jan. 2017. <https://www.youtube.com/watch?v=U-8iUNqUwXg>.

[57]http://www.infowars.com/tech-billionaires-secretly-funding-scientists-to-help-break-out-of-matrix-reality/

[58] http://www.cnn.com/2015/12/02/politics/donald

hoping that was very dry sarcasm, but from further evidence it likely was not. The evidence is that in an attempt to back up a claim he made during his campaign that Muslims cheered in the streets during 9/11 he tweeted out a link to an InfoWars story.[59]

So perhaps the most damaging part of push polling's evolution into fake news, is not that more ordinary people are buying into it, but that now a precedent has been set for candidates to cite it.

---

trump-praises-9-11-truther-alex-jones/
[59]https://twitter.com/realdonaldtrump/status/669672417774694400?lang=en

Flipping Tamaulipas

For this portion of the book we reached out to the President of DIF Reynosa, Carlos Pena. We were interested to see if the transition of power in Tamaulipas was in line with our theory—*the only way to guarantee an eventual loss is to not change*. What we received from Carlos was an incredible tale of an uphill battle against a well established party, all while dealing with obstacles that are unique to the Mexican political landscape. Ultimately, it appears that even in a vastly different political environment the overarching theory does indeed hold. Here is Mr. Pena's story of how the PAN broke the 87 year grip of the PRI in Tamaulipas.

In Tamaulipas, Mexico, violence and illegal activity has become ingrained into the daily lives of the roughly 3.5 million citizens who call the state home. Located in the northeastern corner of Mexico, Tamaulipas is a vast land that covers over 370 kilometers (230 miles) of shared border with the United States. It is an incredible place, and its location has given the state much prosperity in the form of trade and business dealings with its Northern neighbor, the United States. However, its proximity to the U.S. has also allowed the proliferation of criminal organizations who deal in the trafficking of narcotics, money, arms, and people. Rather than being recognized for its vast manufacturing sector, agricultural output, or rich oil fields, Tamaulipas is mainly known for its record-breaking abilities in areas most Tamaulipecans would prefer to forget about. Today, Tamaulipas has more than 5,583[60] individuals missing (the highest number in Mexico), the highest rate of kidnapping[61] in the country, and the top spot in petroleum theft[62] and possession of illegal weapons by minors in Mexico.[63] The murder rates in Tamaulipas are not considered the highest in Mexico only because individuals that are "disappeared" cannot be counted towards the murder rate. Tamaulipas is also notorious for the violent massacres that occur throughout the state—many of which have made international headlines—like the brutal murder of 72 Central American migrants by the Zetas cartel in 2010.

The security crisis in Tamaulipas accelerated in 2010 after the Zetas cartel, long considered the armed branch of the Gulf Cartel, defected from the Gulf Cartel. A violent war immediately ensued across

---

[60]http://www.insightcrime.org/news-briefs/disappearance-statistics-highlights-turmoil-in-tamaulipas

[61] http://www.forbes.com.mx/los-10-estados-con-mas-secuestros-en-mexico/#gs.IGt7ODI

[62]http://www.insightcrime.org/news-briefs/oil-theft-in-mexico-up-44-percent

[63]http://www.excelsior.com.mx/nacional/2016/01/03/1066578

the state. The cartels disputed territory in every corner of the Tamaulipas, causing thousands of deaths and spreading terror and violence to the entire region. Turmoil within different sectors of the population began to grow as the developing security crisis scared off foreign investment, hindered business, increased unemployment, and pushed thousands of citizens outside of Tamaulipas. The wave of migration out of Tamaulipas occurred despite the recent energy reform in which Tamaulipas was projected to significantly benefit from as a primary petroleum producer. The reform, which promised to bring thousands of jobs and heavy investment to the state, has not been enough to stop Tamaulipecans from moving North to the United States or to other states within Mexico like Nuevo Leon or San Luis Potosi to flee from violence.

Those who have opted to remain in the region—many without a choice—continue to struggle with the widespread terror. Not even the well-protected political elite receive mercy; in 2010 the *Partido Revolucionario Institucional* (PRI) candidate for governor, Rodolfo Torre Cantu, and 5 of his collaborators were assassinated days before the gubernatorial election took place. (Mr. Torre Cantu won the election post-mortem since his name still appeared on the ballot). Mr.Torre Cantu's assassination came as no surprise to Tamaulipecans given the dirty (and dangerous) nature of politics in the region. Today, two former governors of Tamaulipas, Tomas Yarrington[64] (1998-2004) and Eugenio Hernandez Flores[65] (2004-2010), are currently listed as fugitives by the U.S. Department of Justice on money laundering charges in relation to bribes received by cartels.[66] Mexico's Attorney General's office has an apprehension order against Yarrington but has curiously not issued one against Hernandez Flores. Even more intriguing was Hernandez Flores' public appearance during Election Day on June 5, 2016. During this appearance he gave an interview claiming that the PRI would win Tamaulipas and represented the best choice for Tamaulipecans; all this while being a fugitive from the U.S. Department of Justice.

---

[64]https://archives.fbi.gov/archives/sanantonio/press-releases/2013/former-governor-of-state-of-tamaulipas-mexico-indicted-in-the-southern-district-of-texas

[65]https://www.justice.gov/usao-sdtx/pr/former-tamaulipas-governor-indicted-money-laundering-scheme-brother-law

[66]http://www.expressnews.com/news/local/article/Former-Mexican-border-governor-indicted-6337757.php

67

The Surge of the PAN

The track record of infamous Tamaulipas governors and public officials tarnished the reputation of the PRI in the state, which had held power in Tamaulipas since 1929. Though Mexico has long been thought to have become liberated from the PRI's authoritarian rule, many regions of Mexico, like Tamaulipas, had remained under the PRI's firm grip even after the presidential victory of *Partido Accion Nacional* (PAN) candidate Vicente Fox in 2000. June 5, 2016 marked the end of 87 years of the PRI's historic uninterrupted rule in Tamaulipas. Opposition to the PRI in Tamaulipas had been growing for years, but the PRI's support base remained strong due to the control exercised by their impressive political

---

[67] Image of the assassination of PRI's candidate for Governor, Egidio Torre Cantu.

machine. The effectiveness of their statewide machinery slowly dwindled as the PAN, operating as the strongest opposition in the state, began organizing a grassroots movement that mobilized citizens and ultimately concluded in a victorious unprecedented election with over 50% of the vote in favor.

68

The ousting of the PRI was long overdue in Tamaulipas. The PRI was able to retain power prior to 2016 by aligning itself with different syndicates and associations in various sectors and by maintaining a centralized party structure. Mexico's Workers, Petroleum, Railroad, Farmers, and the Teacher's Syndicate (the largest one in Latin America) have always been pillars of the PRI's political machine, the most organized in of all Mexico. For decades, the PRI has sought to benefit the leading members of their political apparatus, a small number of political oligarchs within the party

---

68 PAN Tamaulipas in their closing campaign event.

that maintain full control. Other parties have tried to copy the PRI's political structure by centralizing their grassroots movements, but have been ineffective because the sustainability of such a structure can only be maintained by an incumbent political party. In other words, without the governmental base, the PRI's political structure would collapse.

The PRI's centralized political structure, though highly efficient and organized, had excluded millions of Mexicans and Tamaulipecans for decades. In Tamaulipas the opposition, aka the PAN, was able to tap into the groups that had been historically excluded by the PRI and who had long been struggling with social, political, and economic turmoil. The efforts to form an alliance with these sectors proved to be vital in driving the PRI out of power for the first time in 87 years. Communicating and listening to electors was key in forming the alliances that won the campaign. A grassroots political structure, social media, polls, and good old door-to-door campaigning played a significant role in the changing of parties in Tamaulipas. The PAN continues to use these strategies today to remain close to its citizens and to maintain the grassroots movement that brought them to power.

PAN's Grassroots Strategy

For political parties, a strong and organized electoral structure is vital to successfully compete with other political movements. Without an electoral structure the future of a party is lost. Party structure is key when voter turnout is low. In the case of Tamaulipas, voter turnout has historically been one of the lowest ones—5th lowest out of 32 states[69]—in the country. In 2012 during the last Presidential election, voter turnout was around 55%, far below the 62.06% national average.[70] In elections with low turnout, a party's political structure becomes the most important factor in an election outcome. For the PAN in Tamaulipas, the party structure in place in 2016 represented a way to compete with the PRI for the first time in 87 years.

In 2015 the PAN in Tamaulipas began working on a decentralized grassroots political structure that gave a voice to thousands of citizens in Tamaulipas. The decentralized structure also served to diminish the possibility of betrayals within the PAN that could strike deadly blows to the party. Prior

---

[69] http://www.ine.mx/docs/IFE-v2/DECEYEC/DECEYEC-EstudiosInvestigaciones/InvestigacionIFE/Estudio_Censal_Participacion_Ciudadana_2012.pdf

[70] http://www.ine.mx/docs/IFE-v2/DECEYEC/DECEYEC-EstudiosInvestigaciones/InvestigacionIFE/Estudio_Censal_Participacion_Ciudadana_2012.pdf

to this party reform any opponent could potentially convince (and had done so in previous elections) a party oligarch to switch sides and severely affect the party structure enough to impact the results of an election. Under this new decentralized scheme any betrayal within the party structure would be insignificant to the election results.

The PAN's structure depended on a division of the party's resources into the 22 local electoral districts in Tamaulipas. Under these districts, 4 or 5 councils were formed to represent each district (the exact number depending on the population of the district). Each council was formed by members of different *colonias* or neighborhoods within the council's jurisdiction. Each council was constructed by leaders of over 30 neighborhoods. Neighborhood committees were organized by citizens and helped expose the issues within each neighborhood. These committees were in charge of understanding and exposing the neighborhood's grievances and the councils were to address each committee's concerns. Under this new grassroots political structure the PAN's candidates listened to every committee and council, effectively engaging thousands of Tamaulipecans. Common citizens formed part of these committees and party affiliation was not required in order to participate. Even members of other political parties took part and actively participated within the grassroots structure. The openness and inclusive platform created by the PAN engaged the thousands of Tamaulipecans that had been marginalized by the PRI for close to 87 years. The new political network created thousands of new leaders within the PAN's structure.

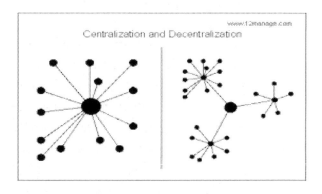

The outreach structures used during elections were maintained during the new administrations in Tamaulipas. The same neighborhood committees and councils formed during the 2016 campaign have continued to collaborate with the new government on various policy issues. These councils participate in the decision-making process and keep the government informed about the most pressing needs of the communities. Public servants have built close relationships with the committees so as to adequately and directly address the needs of the population.

The PAN also received significant support from a network of many civil society organizations and private sector organizations. From healthcare providers, teachers, farmers, animal advocacy groups, and associations like the Lions and Rotary clubs, the PAN received widespread support from a number of civil society organizations, and consequently built its platform to address many of their issues. This network, although not controlled by the PAN, was instrumental in the PAN's victory. Today, the Tamaulipecan government has welcomed the input of these organizations by inviting them to collaborate with the administration on the construction of new policies and the *Plan de Desarrollo Estatal* (State Development Project). The State Development Project is the plan that will dictate the future of investment in security, infrastructure, education, social programs, and public policy by the state government. These collaboration forums have built a more inclusive and engaged civic population in Tamaulipas, and are a complete turnaround from the ways the PRI governed.

Polling

Like in the United States, political polling in Mexico has come to play a significant role in campaigns in the 21st century. Today, polling is a regular tool used by parties to gain insight on citizen opinion and campaign results. Polls allow politicians and candidates to better understand the electorate and communicate their messages with clarity and efficiency. In early 2016, hundreds of polls measured Tamaulipecans' political preferences and views/priorities on the issues each party presented in their platform. In late 2015, polling between the PAN and PRI in the state of Tamaulipas marked a statistical tie.[71]

Political analysts predicted a close race, and understood that the Tamaulipecans priorities lied in restoring peace/reducing violence in the state and improving the economy.[72] According to polling, more than 50% of Tamaulipecans believed that violence/security was the most important issue in the state of Tamaulipas, the second most important issue was the economy with 25%, and in a distant third came combating corruption within the government with 17%.[73] The PAN campaigned on the return of peace and prosperity to the state, and on bringing to justice those responsible for the violence. Maki Ortiz,

[71]http://www.sdpnoticias.com/local/tamaulipas/2015/12/08/encuesta-tamaulipas-empatados-francisco-cabeza-de-vaca-y-baltazar-hinojosa

[72]http://consulta.mx/index.php/estudios-e-investigaciones/elecciones-mexico/item/863-tamaulipas-como-votaron-sus-ciudadanos-analisis-de-la-encuesta-de-salida

[73]http://consulta.mx/index.php/estudios-e-investigaciones/elecciones-mexico/item/863-tamaulipas-como-votaron-sus-ciudadanos-analisis-de-la-encuesta-de-salida

mayor of Reynosa (the largest city in the state of Tamaulipas) believed "Tamaulipecans were tired of living in a state where every year thousands were murdered, kidnapped or persecuted by violence."

The PAN was the first party in Tamaulipas to heavily campaign on restoring peace in the state largely because of the threat that the cartels pose to parties and politicians. Talking about restoring peace in the state is an affront to criminal organizations. Considering the murder of the PRI's candidate for governor in 2010, restoring the peace and security of Tamaulipas became a bold platform to run on by any party or candidate. Parties not only live in fear of the cartels, but in some cases have also sought to downplay the security crisis. For many years the PRI has been accused of hiding violent events in the state, pretending that violence has only manifested itself in isolated events. Despite the attempts of the PRI to cover up the violence, the citizens of Tamaulipas were well aware of the security crisis and wanted a party and candidates that would finally acknowledge the brutal reality they faced every day.

The PRI, on the other hand, focused on a negative campaign that sought to tarnish the reputation of many of the PAN's candidates including PAN's candidate for governor and current governor of Tamaulipas, Francisco Garcia Cabeza de Vaca. TV

and Radio ads claiming that Mr. Cabeza de Vaca had
received money from cartels, had been incarcerated
for gun theft in the United States, had been involved
in an assassination attempt, and had stolen millions of
pesos in his administration in the city of Reynosa
were seen and heard every couple of minutes across
the state of Tamaulipas during 2016 electoral process.

[74]While at the national level combating
corruption is one of the biggest concerns for most
citizens, in Tamaulipas combating corruption,
although important, was not a priority for most
Tamaulipecans, particularly in comparison to
returning peace to the state. The PRI's anti-corruption
campaign efforts were ultimately ineffective in
changing the socio-political landscape during the

---

[74] Governor Garcia Cabeza de Vaca picture after being
detained in Mcallen, Texas in 1986.

electoral process. The PRI's political strategists failed to understand the local concerns of Tamaulipecans. A phrase by Tip O'Neill, the former U.S. Speaker of the House, "all politics is local" helps us understand the failed strategy of the PRI. Tamaulipecans were less concerned with corruption and more concerned with restoring peace and prosperity in the state. Citizens ultimately decided that only the PAN could make a difference in regards to this issue. The PRI eventually responded by strengthening its efforts to reach out to civilians with solutions to stop the violence and proposals to create more jobs in the state, but by then it was too late.

Social Media

In Tamaulipas, only 60 percent of the homes have access to the internet (access to internet is 39.2 percent across Mexico).[75] Consequently, most political advertisement continues to be done through radio and television. Despite traditional radio and television propaganda, social media has become fundamental in motivating the younger demographics to vote. 18-29 year olds make up one of largest demographic groups in Mexico but their participation in Mexican elections is minimal. In 2016, Tamaulipas became an outlier in young voter turnout. Tamaulipas

---

[75]http://www.inegi.org.mx/saladeprensa/aproposito/201
6/internet2016_0.pdf

had over 27% of participation of this important demographic, much higher than the national average of 22%.[76] Moreover, the difference between the PAN and PRI among young adults was of 20 percentage points, making 18-29 year olds the most important "difference makers" within voting demographics in Tamaulipas for the 2016 election.[77]

Another important factor that PAN's political analysts took into account was the percentage of social media users by platform: Facebook, Instagram, Twitter, Snapchat, etc. In Mexico 98.8% of social media users use Facebook, 25% use Instagram, 23% use Twitter, and less than 10% use Youtube, Snapchat, Pinterest, or Google.[78] Having taken all these factors into account it would only make sense that most political social media activity during the campaign took place on Facebook, Instagram, and Twitter. These social media websites allowed candidates to express their views, listen to harsh criticism, and accuse one another of money laundering, corruption, drug trafficking, and even

[76]http://consulta.mx/index.php/estudios-e-investigaciones/elecciones-mexico/item/863-tamaulipas-como-votaron-sus-ciudadanos-analisis-de-la-encuesta-de-salida

[77]http://consulta.mx/index.php/estudios-e-investigaciones/elecciones-mexico/item/863-tamaulipas-como-votaron-sus-ciudadanos-analisis-de-la-encuesta-de-salida

[78] http://www.elfinanciero.com.mx/tech/numero-de-usuarios-de-redes-sociales-crece-18-en-mexico.html

attempted murder. While most parties dedicated themselves to accusing the PAN candidates of these and many others crimes, the PAN campaign committed themselves to polling users and understanding their views on what had to change in Tamaulipas.

Social media allowed candidates to express their policies and concerns about the future of the state. PAN candidates such as Maki Ortiz and many others live-streamed on Facebook to answer questions from citizens and directly responded to messages or comments from Reynosa's citizens throughout the campaign. Although risky, because livestream exercises can be easily sabotaged by opponents, they effectively create a direct link between voters and candidates. While many candidates and parties were not able to understand the biggest concerns—security & violence—for the Tamaulipecan population, the PAN candidates used social media to study the issues the Tamaulipecans were most concerned about and consequently addressed those concerns.

Today, social media plays a significant role in campaigning, and will become more important to determining elections in Mexico as access to the internet is brought to more households. All of the polling, sharing, liking, commenting, and uploading would not have been possible without the cyber armies each party hired during the campaign. The large investment of resources and personnel dedicated to social media was a testament to the importance parties such as the PAN place in social media to have a significant role in their interaction with the public.

Old Fashioned Door to Door

Direct contact between electors and candidates is, was, and always will be the most effective manner to build political support within a constituency. Participating in debates, making Town Hall appearances with constituents, and conducting personal house visits to electors' homes are particularly vital for candidates in countries where Internet access to a large portion of the population is limited, such as Mexico. Such campaign strategies are the only way millions of Mexicans are able to know and understand the views of a party or candidate. Candidate debates and town hall hearings allow constituents to compare and contrast the different political options available, but these democratic exercises could hinder a candidate's possibilities of winning. Visiting constituents in the intimacy of their home, however, will more than likely always help a candidate or increase a party's sympathizers. Mexico's politicians have long understood this: it is common for candidates of all parties to visit citizens in the privacy of their homes during campaigns. All

Mexicans have seen political parties inundate small neighborhoods with campaign stops so grandiose they almost rival city parades: full of banners, music, speeches, and free giveaways. For the candidates, ambitious campaigning means long hours under the sun to ensure every corner of every neighborhood is visited. Candidates also endure insults, threats, and in many cases even violence from citizens. Extravagant campaigning wears many candidates down, but it remains the most effective way for aspiring office holders to communicate political messages and to truly know and understand the pressing needs of the electorate.

While campaigning within communities in Tamaulipas, candidates must strive to 1) visualize and focus in on a single message that connects to the electors, is interesting to the electors, and is suitable for a political campaign. 2) Remain conscious of the distribution of the population and their political preference among different districts (understand the lay of the land). 3) Plan a strategy that extends the chosen political message to as many homes as possible. (A strict adherence to this three-step strategy in Tamaulipas is easier said than done, because there are so many things that can happen during a campaign to affect the decisions and conduct of candidates.)

A strategy traditionally used by parties is to coordinate campaign stops where popular politicians affiliated with the party and the general area accompany the aspiring candidate during his or her appearances. The joint campaign stops are not common and typically reserved for concentrated areas which may or may not cover the majority of the population.

These old strategies ultimately failed, as demonstrated by the recent 2016 campaigns of Tamaulipas. In line with the theme of this book, the lack of change in a campaign is how a campaign, candidate, or political party will eventually lose, whether it is a presidential election in the United States or a local election in Mexico.

The 2016 campaign season included the election of council members, mayors, local representatives, and the governor. Many parties prioritized organizing joint appearances with all the party's candidates over numerous appearances throughout the region. The winning party (PAN) opted to cover as much ground as possible by dividing cities into different sectors so that all candidates would spend the majority of their time visiting as many sectors as possible and thus covering the majority of the state. All of the PAN candidates spent 40% of their campaign visiting homes, businesses, supermarkets, and restaurants in Tamaulipas' 43 municipalities. The extensive campaigning allowed the PAN's message to spread to far more homes and citizens in Tamaulipas than the PRI's message—largely explaining the PAN's victory over the PRI.

Campaigning while Governing

Mexico's political dynamic is not typically observed in other areas of the world due to the fact that Mexico holds major political campaigns every single year. In 2015, for example, federal representatives were selected, in 2016 mayors, local representatives, and governors in 12 states were selected, in 2017 multiple governors with their respective congresses and mayors will be selected, and in 2018 local elections will be held alongside the mother of all elections, the Presidency of Mexico. The electoral climate forces all parties to operate in election mode at all times, working to gain new supporters or retain the party's current sympathizers. In response to this electoral demand, the PAN has created the *Programa de Accion Comunitaria (PAC)* (Community Action Program). PAC allows members of society to directly interact with PAN leaders and the PAN platform. In addition to bringing together representatives from the PAN and the community, this project also gives opportunities for community work such as cleaning streets, ponds, and parks together.

Moreover, party leaders/government officials
learn and recognize a citizen's needs and connect
them to the corresponding agency forming credibility
and trust between the party and society, resulting in
the party achieving presence within society and
attracting sympathizers. To this end, while this is a
feature unique to Mexican politics, the initiative to
provide new methods of outreach while governing is
the PAN's way of innovating to ensure it continues to
increase the quality of life for all Tamaulipecans.

Beat the Goat

The history of elections spanning from the United States to Mexico show us, there is no set way to win a campaign. There is no bright line or secret key to winning the local mayoral race or the US presidency. The keys to winning an election appear to be short lived at best as the world of campaigning evolves. However, there is a set way to lose an election that all campaigns should keep an eye out for—*failing to change*.

A campaign that does not change is destined to lose eventually. A campaign may have the political machine strong enough to keep a grasp on a few election cycles. A campaign may have the data to understand its community today, the institutional organization to mobilize its supporters, and a method of outreach that has won before—but it may not tomorrow. Eventually another campaign will exploit its lack of change in one or multiple areas.

Every day there are people innovating new methods of understanding the electorate, whether it is new methods of gathering new data, using big data, or new ways of interpreting the data we already have access to.

Every day there are new methods and initiatives to increase the efficiency and effectiveness of organizing, whether it is optimizing the organization of the campaign workers or the voters themselves.

Every day there is a new way being developed to reach out to voters, from Facebook sponsored posts to building a connection with humor.

So while there is no guaranteed way to win a campaign, there is a way to lose, and campaigns that ignore the power of innovation and change for long enough may find themselves losing an election to a beer drinking goat.

Made in the USA
San Bernardino, CA
22 February 2017